MW00805692

# It's... an Elephant

Om
KIDZ
**An imprint of Om Books International**

First Published in 2019 by

Om KIDZ | Om **Books International**

**Corporate & Editorial Office**
A-12, Sector 64, Noida 201 301
Uttar Pradesh, India
Phone: +91 120 477 4100
Email: editorial@ombooks.com
Website: www.ombooksinternational.com

**Sales Office**
107, Ansari Road, Darya Ganj
New Delhi 110 002, India
Phone: +91 11 4000 9000
Email: sales@ombooks.com
Website: www.ombooks.com

© Om Books International 2019

ISBN: 978-93-86410-46-7

Printed in India

10 9 8 7 6 5 4 3 2 1

ALL RIGHTS RESERVED. No part of this book
may be reproduced or transmitted in any
form by any means, electronic or mechanical,
including photocopying and recording, or by
any information storage and retrieval system,
except as may be expressly permitted in writing
by the publisher.

# Contents

# WHO ARE YOU?

Hello, I am an elephant. I belong to the Elephantidae family. I am the largest living animal on land.

## Scientific Name

*Loxodonta*

of the African Elephant

## My Young Ones
My babies are known as calves.

We have a long trunk, thick legs, huge fan-shaped ears and a large head. Our body hair is rough. We are greyish to brown in colour. We also have pointed tusks.

## Cows and Bulls

Female elephants are known as cows while male elephants are called bulls.

# HOW BIG ARE YOU?

Female Asian Elephant

The Asian elephant is 3.5 m tall and weighs around 5500 kg. The African elephant weighs almost 8000 kg and is 3 to 4 m tall.

## Long Tusks

The tusks of African elephants can grow up to 10 ft in length.

We eat roots, barks, bamboo, twigs, shrubs, fruits, vegetables, grain and grasses. Hay forms a major part of our diet.

Big Vic, an elephant bull in Mana Pools National Park, Zimbabwe.

## Like Size, Like Appetite

Our appetite matches our huge size. A hungry adult elephant can eat up to 136 kg of food in one day.

# WHAT A LONG NOSE YOU HAVE!

A new word to learn

Dexterous - skilful

It's called a trunk! Our trunk is a combination of our nose and upper lip. We have nostrils at the tip of our trunk. While an African elephant's trunk can stretch more, an Asian elephant's trunk is much more **dexterous**.

## Majestic Trunks

Our trunk is the most versatile part of our body. We can lift loads of up to 250 kg with our trunk. An adult elephant's trunk weighs around 130 kg.

We mainly use our trunk to breathe, smell, drink water, bathe and pick up things. We suck water through our trunk and pour it into our mouth or spray it on ourselves.

# WHAT DO YOU DO WITH YOUR TRUNK?

## Trunk Shake

When we meet, we may use our trunks to touch each other. Sometimes we even twist our trunks in a 'trunk-shake', which is similar to the human handshake.

We use our strong tusks to defend ourselves, pick up things, pull out tree barks, dig up roots from the ground and for several other purposes.

A new word to learn

Sensitive - quick to detect

## Sensitive Trunks

Our trunks are very **sensitive** and they contain around 40,000 different muscles.

We are mostly found in forests and savannas. However, we can also survive in swamps, highlands and deserts. Many of us are found in captivity.

## Matriarchal Head

Elephant herds are led by an older and experienced female elephant.

# HOW DO YOU COMMUNICATE?

We make two kinds of sounds—low and high. The low sounds include snorting, growling, roaring and the rolling growl. The high sounds include crying, trumpeting, trumping, barking and the gruff cry.

When we sense danger, we raise our trunk and rotate it in the air. We also trumpet, to raise an alarm and inform the other elephants about the approaching danger.

# CAN YOU SING?

A new word to learn

Rumbling - Continous deep sound

Yes. We make **rumbling** sounds that are too soft for humans to hear. We sing to keep our herd together. This also helps us find mates.

## Herd Size

We live in herds consisting of 10 or more elephants.

Yes. We have six sets of cheek teeth but all of them do not come out at the same time.

## Tooth Loss

It is said that an elephant can die due to tooth loss as that can lead to starvation.

# ARE YOU A SOCIAL ANIMAL?

Yes, we are mostly social animals. We live in herds. However, in the wild, it is easy to find adult male elephants who have been driven out of their family groups. A herd mostly consists of related female elephants and their young ones.

# ARE YOU AN INTELLIGENT ANIMAL?

Yes. We are one of the most intelligent animals on Earth. Our brain size is larger than that of any other land animal. We have excellent memory. We can recognize ourselves in the mirror.

## Thick Skinned

Elephants have very thick skin. The skin on their head and back is almost 2 to 4 cm thick.

# WHAT IS YOUR LIFESPAN?

We have a lifespan of about 60 years, when in the wild. However, we can survive up to 80 years or more, when in captivity.

## Migration

We migrate seasonally depending upon the availability of food and water.

# HOW BIG IS YOUR NEWBORN CALF?

A newborn elephant calf is about 3.3 ft tall and can weigh up to 100 kg.

## Poor Eyesight at Birth

Newborn calves have poor eyesight at birth. Their eyesight improves as they grow older. They can identify their mother by her scent, sound and touch.

CAN YOU RUN?

Our fast-paced movement is called rushing. We can move at speeds of almost 25 miles per hour.

# African Elephant vs Asian Elephant

Asian and African elephants can be distinguished based on the size of their ears. African elephants have longer ears, which are shaped like the continent of Africa. Also, African elephants have round heads and the top of their head looks like a single dome. Asian elephants, on the other hand, have a twin-domed head. An African elephant's skin is more wrinkled than that of an Asian elephant's.

Twin Dome

Single Dome

African Elephant

Asian Elephant

# ACTIVITY TIME

## PAPER ELEPHANT CRAFT

Things You'll Need

- Grey and white cardstock paper
- Glue bottle
- Scale
- Pencil
- Scissors
- Googly eyes

Take a rectangular piece of grey cardstock paper and fold it into half.

Now, place the image of an elephant over the paper and draw an outline. Cut out the outline.

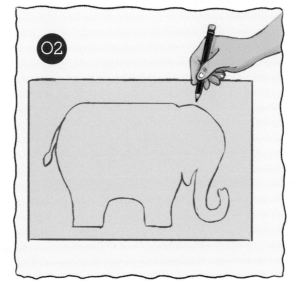

Open the fold of the cut-out and paste glue all over the upper half of the elephant's body.

Now fold a piece of grey cardstock paper and cut out huge ears for the elephant. Now make a small cut at the back of the elephant's neck and stick the ears.

Using white cardstock paper, cut out the tusks of the elephant. Make a small cut below the elephant's trunk and paste the tusks.

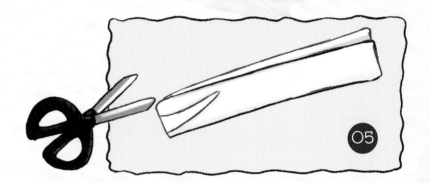

Now, paste the googly eyes and voila, your paper elephant is ready!

The baby elephant is hungry. Help it reach the bananas.

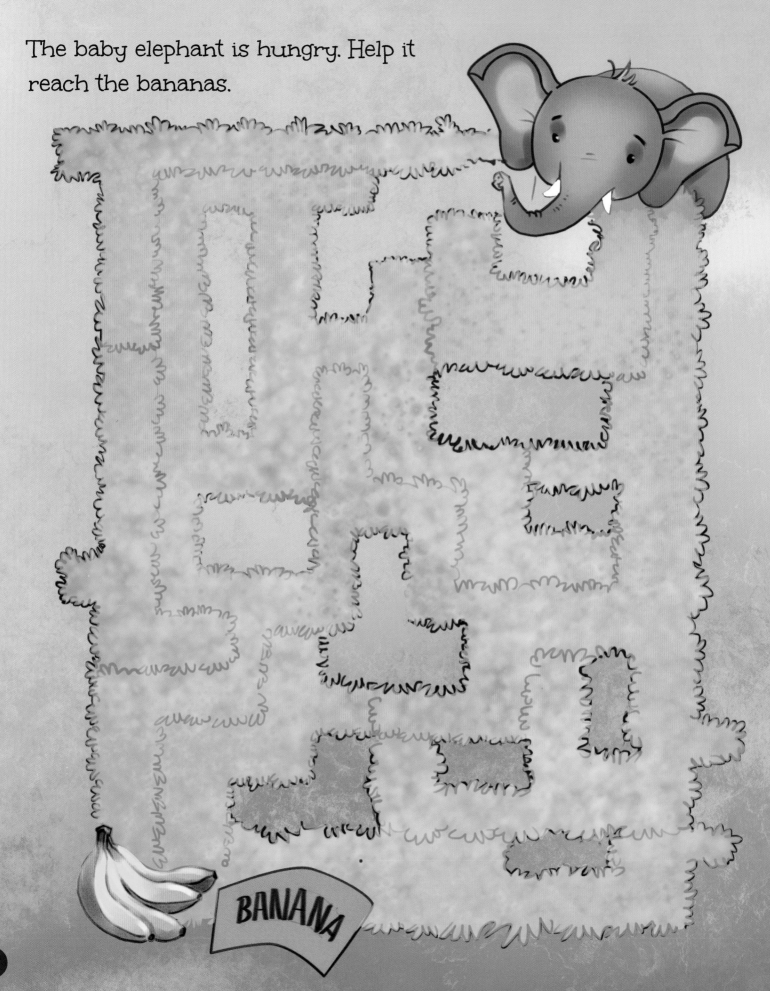

BANANA